MEN, WOMEN & MONEY

HIS

MEN, WOMEN & MONEY

HIS

A couples' guide to navigating
money better, together

Shaunti and Jeff Feldhahn
presented by brightpeak®

BETHANY HOUSE
a division of Baker Publishing Group
www.BethanyHouse.com

Published by Bethany House Publishers
11400 Hampshire Avenue South
Bloomington, Minnesota 55438
www.bethanyhouse.com

Bethany House Publishers is a division of
Baker Publishing Group, Grand Rapids, Michigan

Printed in the United States of America

ISBN 978-0-7642-3261-9

Unless otherwise indicated, Scripture quotations are from the Holy Bible, New Inter-
national Version®. NIV®. Copyright © 1973, 1978, 1984, 2011 by Biblica, Inc.™ Used by
permission of Zondervan. All rights reserved worldwide. www.zondervan.com

Scripture quotations marked esv are from The Holy Bible, English Standard Version®
(ESV®), copyright © 2001 by Crossway, a publishing ministry of Good News Publishers.
Used by permission. All rights reserved. ESV Text Edition: 2011

Scripture quotations marked nasb are from the New American Standard Bible®, copyright © 1960, 1962, 1963, 1968, 1971, 1972, 1973, 1975, 1977, 1995 by The Lockman Foundation.
Used by permission. (www.Lockman.org)

Scripture quotations marked nlt are from the Holy Bible, New Living Translation, copyright © 1996, 2004, 2015 by Tyndale House Foundation. Used by permission of Tyndale
House Publishers, Inc., Carol Stream, Illinois 60188. All rights reserved.

Cover design by Olivia Herrick

Jeff and Shaunti: To our amazing team: Thanks for investing your talents with us, and going the extra mile in time, encouragement, prayer, and coffee.

brightpeak: To our members as you journey down the path of living with contentment, confidence, and generosity in your relationships and your finances.

TABLE OF CONTENTS

IN EACH SESSION YOU WILL:

- Watch a 25-minute video
- Talk through some discussion questions and what each session means for you
- Understand your spouse and feel understood like never before
- Take advantage of the extended experience, if you'd like

GETTING STARTED

Welcome to Men, Women, and Money!
We are so honored and excited
that you've chosen to do this video
discussion series. At brightpeak, we are
super excited to be able to partner with
Shaunti and Jeff to bring you this truly
game-changing information.

If you're having a tough time navigating money as a couple, you're not alone. As we at brightpeak research this topic, we're finding that more than raising kids, managing the in-laws, or even sex, MONEY is the number one cause of stress in relationships. Yet most of the time, the stress and conflict isn't just about the money itself—it's about other factors running under the surface that are being triggered by money. One of those factors is the very real difference between men and women. These differences lead to misunderstandings, stress, distance, guilt, shame and even divorce.

The great news is that even though men and women are built differently, there are consistent principles in how most men and most women think, feel and act when it comes to money. This series was created to be your starting point to learn about your spouse or significant other, and begin to see how these deeper factors affect your relationship with love and money.

In this video discussion experience, you'll get a seat at the table with best-selling authors and social researchers Jeff and Shaunti Feldhahn. For more than 16 years, Jeff and Shaunti have been studying the differences between men and women. Their research has helped hundreds of thousands of couples gain a better understanding of how their partners are wired and what they can do about it. If you'd like to learn more about their research and their methodology, visit www.shaunti.com/research.

brightpeak is a not-for-profit organization with a refreshingly holistic approach to personal finances. Our mission is to help couples live with confidence and generosity in their relationships and their finances. We work with many churches, community groups and individual couples—and we're thrilled you're joining us here. You can learn more at www.brightpeak.com

Now, we've joined forces to offer you this series that gives you the understanding you'll need to grow deeper in your relationship while navigating your finances.

HOW TO USE THIS BOOK

Have you ever wished that your spouse came with a manual? That would be fantastic! Well, our goal with this guide is for you to have the information and tools you need to create your own manual for working well with each other as you manage your money. This guide is yours so please make it your own. Feel free to write in it, dog-ear pages, tape things in it and use it however will serve you best.

IN EACH SESSION YOU WILL:
- Watch a 25-minute video
- Talk through some discussion questions and what each session means for you
- Understand your spouse and feel understood like never before
- Take advantage of the extended experience, if you'd like

CUSTOMIZE THE EXPERIENCE THAT'S RIGHT FOR YOU
Each lesson has a core experience that lasts around 45-60 minutes, depending on how in-depth you get in your conversation. We've also provided three sections of extended experience so that couples or groups can mix and match additional exercises as they see fit.

1. WHAT ARE THEY THINKING? A CASE STUDY
You'll have the opportunity to read a short story about a couple who is working through a money conflict or situation together. Then, you'll take turns putting yourself in the shoes of the other person—and sharing your own reactions. These case studies help you learn the skill of understanding the inner stuff that your partner may be thinking in money-related situations but doesn't know how to say. They also walk you through how to apply it to your own life.

2. GOING DEEPER: ADDITIONAL DISCUSSION QUESTIONS

Also, in each session you can explore more discussion questions that will help you continue to talk through and apply the concepts from the lesson.

3. FAITH FOCUS: BIBLE STUDY

Finally, in each session you can read a section of the Bible and reflect on how that passage of Scripture connects to what you just learned in the lesson.

For example, if you're doing this as part of premarital counseling, you might add the Case Study and a few Going Deeper discussion questions. A group Bible study might add the Faith Focus section. Create the customized experience that is right for you.
Here's a quick look at what the extended experience includes.

Remember: The extended experience is there as a bonus. If you and your spouse choose to stick to the core lesson and not do that bonus stuff, that's great! You should feel really proud of that.

ACCESSING YOUR VIDEOS ONLINE:
To access your videos online go to:
brightpeak.com/menwomenandmoney/videos
Then enter your access code: WSV-234

IF YOU'RE FACILITATING A GROUP

First off, thank you. We're so honored that you're using this content. To begin, each person in your group will need a book. That allows them to log on and create an account to access the audio and video files. All you need to do before each lesson is choose if you're going to stick to the core experience, or if you'd like to add one or more of the bonus exercises.

Here are a couple things to keep in mind as you lead the group:

1. You do NOT need to be the expert. If someone asks a question you don't know the answer to, no big deal. You can say, "Great question! To be honest, I'm not sure. Does anyone in the group have any ideas?"

2. Be yourself. You don't need to pretend like you have it all together. You get to lead by example as you learn about your own spouse or partner and how you might do things differently.

3. Prepare, then go with the flow. Go into each lesson with a plan in mind, but be ready to let it go if a topic comes up that people really want to talk about, or a need comes up that might need attention or prayer. The goal isn't to get through it all no matter what; it's to connect and grow as a group.

A WORD ABOUT WORDS:

Because this series is designed for couples at a variety of stages in their relationship—including many going through a premarital process—throughout this study we will be referring to spouse, significant other, and partner interchangeably.

YOU HIT
A NERVE

MEN AND WOMEN HAVE
DIFFERENT VULNERABILITIES

SESSION ONE

Have you ever given what you thought was a straightforward answer to a question and gotten an unexpectedly intense response? Or said something to your spouse or significant other only to have them snap at you or shut down—leaving you with no idea what just happened? Ever gotten into a money conflict that became an emotional conflict?

Imagine if you had a window into your partner's internal world, so that you could see what was going on and what you could do to support and encourage them. Even better, imagine if they had a window into yours!

In this first session, our experts—Jeff and Shaunti—dive right in to the heart of many emotional reactions and misunderstandings. They've found that a question is running in the background of most men's and women's minds. Understanding the other person's question— and how you can answer it—will prove to be a game changer.

START THE VIDEO FOR THIS LESSON, THEN TAKE NOTES ABOUT WHAT YOU LEARN.

Learn how to access your videos on page 9.

NOT TRUE FOR YOU?

As you will learn, research suggests these patterns are common to most men and women. But there are always exceptions. If your dynamics are different, simply adapt the examples and questions as needed to discuss how these truths apply to you.

EVEN WOMEN IN GOOD
RELATIONSHIPS FEEL THEY
COULD BE JUST A FEW BAD
BLOWUPS AWAY FROM THINGS
GOING SOUTH.

— *FOR MEN ONLY*

HE WOULD GIVE UP FEELING LOVED, IF HE COULD JUST FEEL RESPECTED

"If I had to choose, I would...

74%	**26%**
Rather be alone and unloved	**Rather feel inadequate and disrespected**

National Survey of Men: How Men Think for *For Women Only*. Survey data as of November 17, 2003

NOTES ABOUT YOU

_____

_____

_____

_____

_____

_____

_____

_____

_____

YOUR CHECK-IN

TAKE ONE MINUTE TO REFLECT ON WHAT YOU JUST LEARNED.

HIS On a scale from 1-10, how true (or not true) is this of you? Do you want people to think that you're good at what you do, but sometimes doubt yourself?

HERS Focus and listen as he shares.

SHE REALLY DOES WONDER IF YOU LOVE HER

82%

I regularly/
sometimes feel
insecure in his love
or the relationship

18%

I never feel insecure
about his love or the
relationship

National Survey of Women for *For Men Only*. Survey data as of June 9, 2005

NOTES ABOUT HER

_____

_____

_____

_____

_____

_____

_____

_____

HER CHECK-IN

TAKE ONE MINUTE TO REFLECT ON WHAT YOU JUST LEARNED.

HERS On a scale of 1-10 how true (or not true) is this of you? Do you subconsciously doubt that you're special, beautiful or loved?

HIS Focus and listen as she shares.

WHAT I CAN DO

WHAT I CAN DO TO SUPPORT MY SPOUSE:

_____

_____

_____

_____

_____

WHAT I COULD ASK MY PARTNER TO DO THAT WOULD REALLY HELP ME A LOT:

_____

_____

_____

_____

_____

YOU HIT A NERVE

VIDEO CONTENT REWIND

In this session, we learned that men and women have different vulnerabilities. **Many men secretly wonder, "Do I measure up?"** They are looking to those around them for clues. **Many women wonder, "Am I lovable? Worth something?"** They are similarly looking for signals from those they care about.

Each of these under-the-surface insecurities is a raw nerve that a spouse or partner can hit without meaning to. And money issues can be a major trigger. Making matters worse, **both men and women tend to use money as a patch for that insecurity.** Yet the ultimate antidote they are looking for is the right kind of affirmation from the one who cares for them most.

BRIGHTPEAK.COM/MENWOMENANDMONEY

DISCUSSION QUESTIONS

These questions are designed to allow you to have a private conversation with your partner, and to gain further insights into how you both think and can apply what you've learned from the chapter. If you are doing this with a group, adapt the questions and exercises as needed. (If a group discussion doesn't lead to you and/or your partner fully understanding what each of you thinks, be sure to continue the conversation later, on your own.)

1. Summarize what you heard from your spouse during the check-in moments of this video, and then communicate it back to him or her. Ask, "Do I have that right?" And give them a chance to elaborate or clarify.

2. Share what you wrote in the "What I could ask my partner to do that would really help me a lot" section.

3. In this session, Jeff and Shaunti shared a story about a couple who bought a new truck to replace the wife's old beat-up one—and then had to return it. He felt like a failure; she felt like she had gone back to being the "poor girl." How would you have felt in that situation?

4. Can you think of a money-related interaction with your spouse when you might have been looking for affirmation or respect—but they didn't understand it and hit that raw nerve of insecurity instead? Talk about what you were each feeling during that interaction.

5. Knowing what you know now, how might you each have handled that situation differently? First, share what you think you could have done differently. Then, allow your partner to share how they think that would (or wouldn't) have changed the outcome. Then, switch roles and give your partner a chance to play Monday morning quarterback with a different interaction (or the same one).

NOTES

_____

_____

_____

_____

_____

_____

_____

_____

_____

_____

_____

_____

_____

_____

MY PERSONAL ACTION PLAN

Question	Example	Your Response
What do I already do well in this area?	I am grateful for her empathy (even if I wish she wouldn't spend quite so much money on other people), and I tell her so.	
What do I most need to work on?	I need to have more empathy for her and realize that sometimes when she suggests going out to eat, she sincerely needs to know that I think she is worth the extra money.	
What is one short-term action step I can take to get there? Note: This should be something measurable: "Try harder" is not specific!	For the next two weeks, each time she suggests spending extra money on something, I will stop myself from a knee-jerk answer, and consider whether a need for affirmation might be underneath it. (If it is, hopefully I'll be able to answer more positively, more often.)	

PICK ONE WAY TO STAY ON TRACK

brightpeak's behavioral scientists have identified some effective ways for making healthy habits stick.

Pick ONE to do right now. Put an X in the box when you're done.

☐ **GIVE YOURSELF A "TRIGGER"**
Set your phone to ping you at critical times over the next week to remember your Personal Action Plan. This could be before you get home to get you in the right head space, or at the end of the day to reflect on how things went.

☐ **LINE UP SOME SOCIAL SUPPORT**
Take a photo of your Personal Action Plan, text it to a friend and ask them to check-in with you to see how it's going.

☐ **CELEBRATE THE SMALL WINS**
Keep an eye out for the little differences you see in yourself and your spouse. Stop and celebrate them in a fun way that's meaningful for you. You could treat yourself to a piece of chocolate or brag them up on social #MenWomenandMoney.

☐ **SCHEDULE A LOOK-BACK ON YOUR CALENDAR**
Mark off 20 minutes in your calendar in the coming week to review your notes, Personal Action Plan, or listen to the audio from the session.

☐ **BUILD YOUR OWN**
You know yourself better than anyone. Write down a specific way you'll overcome the obstacle written in your Personal Action Plan.

SPREAD THE WORD

Did someone you know pop into mind that might really benefit from knowing what you just learned? We're on a mission to help couples do money better together so feel free to **send** them **a photo of the "Video Rewind" page**

NOTES

EXTENDED
EXPERIENCE

SESSION ONE

WHAT ARE THEY THINKING?

A CASE STUDY

Ryan and Emily were out of town attending the wedding of Emily's cousin. They were determined to enjoy the short getaway, as money was tight and they were both working extra hours to catch up on their house payments, which were on a private loan from Emily's wealthy parents. Ryan respects how Emily's parents wisely built their self-made wealth, so he had hated the conversation when they'd had to tell his father-in-law that they were in a tough financial spot and might need a little flexibility on their house payments. He was glad that his year-end bonus would finally allow them to catch up. But that was still two months away.

For now, they were looking forward to Emily's cousin's wedding, which was (in keeping with the money rolling around in Emily's family) "black tie optional" at the nicest country club in town. Ryan borrowed a friend's tux, but Emily decided her outfit would be a surprise. She rented a stunning designer gown (no one would ever have to know that she had to return it in a few days!) and spent an hour getting ready.

Before Ryan had a chance to see her, when she was still in the bathroom finishing her hair, Ryan called through the door that it was time to leave, then headed for the car to warm it up. Frustrated, she quickly finished up, and hustled to the car.

As he watched her carefully fold herself into the front seat, he was taken aback, and stammered, "What are you wearing?" As she grinned and told him it was a gown from a well-known designer her mom and sisters loved, his face went tight.

Seeing that he was looking angry instead of admiring, she quickly reassured him, "It's rented! It hardly cost me anything. And they'll never know it." But he didn't look reassured. Instead he said, "I can't believe you didn't ask me first. They know we can't afford a dress like that! You have to tell them it's rented!"

"No way!" Emily said, angry herself now. "That would be so low-class at a wedding like this. You just don't understand my family!"

They both stared straight ahead as the car sped toward the wedding, wondering if they would even be speaking to each other for the rest of the night.

Take turns responding to your respective questions. Listen carefully to each other's responses in light of what you now know about each other's vulnerabilities and internal questions.

HIS Put yourself in Emily's shoes. What would Emily have been thinking as she was getting ready? What was she likely hoping for when her husband saw her all done up? Now consider: What must Emily have felt during the exchange that actually happened?

HERS If you were in Emily's shoes, what would you have been thinking or feeling during each step of that interaction?

HERS Now put yourself in Ryan's shoes. What might Ryan have been thinking about seeing Emily's family—not just right now, but over the last few months? What would he have been hoping for? Now consider: What might he be thinking as he looks at her designer gown?

HIS If you were in Ryan's shoes, what would you have been thinking or feeling during the last few months and as you see Emily's designer gown?

HIS **HERS** What could Ryan and Emily have done differently? If they had, do you think they would have had a happier outcome? Even if nothing else changed, once they arrived at the wedding, could one of them have said or done anything to change the mood? If so, what?

GOING DEEPER
ADDITIONAL DISCUSSION QUESTIONS

If this topic is an area of interest or challenge for you, consider continuing your discussion time. Read through the questions and each pick at least one that you would love your partner to answer or discuss.

HERS Have you ever gone shopping for new clothes, makeup or housewares because you simply wanted to be more beautiful or surround yourself with beautiful things? (Or have you purchased something to make someone else feel better?) How did it make you feel in the moment? Did that feeling last? Why or why not?

HIS **HERS** Can you think of a time when one of you wanted to spend money on something and felt you deserved that purchase, but your spouse didn't want to spend the money? What did you feel at the time? Now that you know a bit more, what do you think they were thinking at the time? How would you like them to handle it the next time a situation like that comes up? Give them a chance to respond and suggest their own solution.

HIS What in your life do you see as a visible example that you have worked hard and used your talents well?

HIS Imagine that on a trusted friend's advice, you invested a significant amount of your family's savings in a particular investment, which turned out to be a scam. All the money was lost, and the scam became public. Which causes you more pain: The fact that you and your family will have to cut way back on your lifestyle while you rebuild your savings? Or that other men you respect now know about this?

NOTES

For You formed my inward parts; You wove me in my mother's womb. I will give thanks to You, for I am fearfully and wonderfully made; Wonderful are Your works, And my soul knows it very well. My frame was not hidden from You, When I was made in secret, And skillfully wrought in the depths of the earth;
Your eyes have seen my unformed substance; And in Your book were all written The days that were ordained for me, When as yet there was not one of them. How precious also are Your thoughts to me, O God! How vast is the sum of them! If I should count them, they would outnumber the sand. When I awake, I am still with You.

PSALM 139:13-18 NASB

I will proclaim the name of the Lord. Oh, praise the greatness of our God! He is the Rock, his works are perfect, and all his ways are just. A faithful God who does no wrong, upright and just is he.

DEUTERONOMY 32:3-4

FAITH FOCUS

BIBLE STUDY

Read the Scripture, and consider the following questions.

1. Read Psalm 139:13-18. Who is David (the psalmist) speaking to?

2. Make a list of the things that David says God has done in creating him.

3. If these things are true of David, are they also true of you?

4. Now read Deuteronomy 32:3-4. When you consider this verse along with the Psalm Scripture, what does that tell you about God's creation of you?

5. Consider those times when you have used money as an antidote to your personal, private insecurity (even if you didn't realize that that was the impetus at the time). The next time you encounter that temptation, how can you draw on this reassurance instead? Brainstorm specific things that you can do, and discuss them with your spouse.

6. Have there been any difficult interactions (whether money-related or not) with your spouse or significant other that you would handle differently based on what you learned in this session? Is there anything that you need to apologize for and ask for forgiveness from your spouse? Do you need to show grace and forgiveness to your spouse for anything (even if he or she does not ask for it)?

NOTES

HOMELAND SECURITY

MEN AND WOMEN LOOK FOR SECURITY DIFFERENTLY

SESSION TWO

Since the last session, what have you noticed as you followed up on your Personal Action Plan? What challenged you? In what ways were you successful?

If you are willing, share you observations with your partner or group.

IN THIS SESSION

In this session, you'll learn what men and women really mean when they talk about security. Jeff and Shaunti will explain how men typically define security as protecting and providing for their families, while women measure security through emotional connection and closeness.

When couples are operating with misconceptions of each other's definition of security, misunderstanding can prevail.

START THE VIDEO FOR THIS LESSON, THEN TAKE NOTES ABOUT WHAT YOU LEARN.

Learn how to access the videos on page 9.

NOT TRUE FOR YOU?

As you will learn, research suggests these patterns are common to most men and women. But there are always exceptions. If your dynamics are different, simply adapt the examples and questions as needed to discuss how these truths apply to you.

WOMEN FEEL SECURE WHEN
THEY SEE THEIR HUSBAND
CHOOSING TO BE AN ACTIVE
PARTICIPANT IN THE LIFE OF
THE HOME, EVEN IF IT MEANS
REWORKING OTHER PRIORITIES.

— *FOR MEN ONLY*

TIME MEN SPEND THINKING ABOUT PROVIDING FOR THEIR FAMILIES

71%

Are conscious of it often or most of the time

20%

Say it's occasionally in the back of their minds

6%

Only think about it when they're unemployed or facing financial challenges

3%

Never think about it

National Survey of Men: How Men Think for *For Women Only*. Survey data as of November 17, 2003

NOTES ABOUT YOU

_____

_____

_____

_____

_____

_____

_____

_____

YOUR CHECK-IN

TAKE ONE MINUTE TO REFLECT ON WHAT YOU JUST LEARNED.

━━━━━━━━━

HIS On a scale from 1-10, how true (or not true) is this of you? Is this thought about "will I be able to provide for my family" in the back of your mind? Share an example of when it comes up.

HERS Focus and listen as he shares.

70%

of women would rather their husband consider a job with a lower salary— even if it meant lifestyle changes— than stick with a job that pays well but excessively keeps him away from the family.

National Survey of Women for *For Men Only*. Survey data as of June 9, 2005

NOTES ABOUT HER

_____

_____

_____

_____

_____

_____

_____

_____

HER CHECK-IN

TAKE ONE MINUTE TO REFLECT ON WHAT YOU JUST LEARNED.

HERS On a scale of 1-10 how true (or not true) is this of you? Which do you prioritize: the financial security or emotional security/closeness? Share an example of your prioritizing that.

HIS Focus and listen as she shares.

WHAT I CAN DO

WHAT I CAN DO TO SUPPORT MY SPOUSE:

_____

_____

_____

_____

_____

WHAT I COULD ASK MY PARTNER TO DO THAT WOULD REALLY HELP ME A LOT:

_____

_____

_____

_____

_____

HOMELAND SECURITY

VIDEO CONTENT REWIND

In this session, we learned that men and women define security very differently, and these different definitions often lead to different priorities. Ironically, **even as we try to create security for our spouse as well as ourselves,** we may be focusing on areas that don't matter nearly as much to them—while missing those that do.

For most men, the sense of needing to provide is a constant preoccupation—yet he wouldn't have it any other way. He wants to provide for and protect his wife and children. Yet, running through his **subconscious is the ever-present question, "Are we going to be okay financially, as a family?"** So a man is often willing to sacrifice his time with the family in order to put in the hours at work and do whatever he needs to do to provide financial security.

For most women, the desire for emotional security and closeness is deep and constant. In fact, most (although not all) would rather have less financial security if that was what it took to get more of him—his presence, his time, his attention—in the life of the family. She wants emotional security more than financial security and measures emotional security by her connection with him. If he is constantly working, she feels disconnected; she feels secure when he makes spending time with her a priority.

BRIGHTPEAK.COM/MENWOMENANDMONEY

DISCUSSION QUESTIONS

These questions are designed to allow you to have a private conversation with your partner, and to gain further insights into how you both think and can apply what you've learned from the chapter. If you are doing this with a group, adapt the questions and exercises as needed. (If a group discussion doesn't lead to you and/or your partner fully understanding what each of you thinks, be sure to continue the conversation later, on your own.)

1. Summarize what you heard from your partner during the check-in moments of this video, and then communicate it back to him or her. Ask, "Do I have that right?" And give them a chance to elaborate or clarify.

2. Share what you wrote in the "What I could ask my partner to do that would really help me a lot" section.

3. In this session, Jeff and Shaunti shared stories (including a very personal one) about a husband's compulsion to provide—even if it means long hours away—and the impact that has on a wife's need for emotional connectedness. Were you able to relate, or are your patterns different? How would you have felt in any of those situations?

4. Think of a disagreement with your spouse or significant other that you believe shows how you each view security and providing. What were your feelings in that interaction at the time? Is there anything you better understand about yourself and your partner now?

5. Knowing what you know now, how might you each have handled that situation differently at the time to create a better outcome? First, each of you share what you think you could have done better. Take turns weighing in on whether you think those suggested changes might have helped the outcome (or not).

NOTES

MY PERSONAL ACTION PLAN

Question	Example	Your Response
What do I already do well in this area?	I dedicate Sundays to family time.	
What do I most need to work on?	Making family a priority by avoiding taking on so many optional shifts, and making it to the kids' activities.	
What is one short-term action step I can take to get there? Note: This should be something measurable: "Try harder" is not specific!	This semester I will take on no more than one extra shift a week, and I'll check my schedule in advance to be sure I take shifts that allow me to attend all of my daughter's swim meets.	

PICK ONE WAY TO STAY ON TRACK

brightpeak's behavioral scientists have identified some effective ways for making healthy habits stick.

Pick ONE to do right now. Put an X in the box when you're done.

☐ **GIVE YOURSELF A "TRIGGER"**
Set your phone to ping you at critical times over the next week to remember your Personal Action Plan. This could be before you get home to get you in the right head space, or at the end of the day to reflect on how things went.

☐ **LINE UP SOME SOCIAL SUPPORT**
Take a photo of your Personal Action Plan, text it to a friend and ask them to check-in with you to see how it's going.

☐ **CELEBRATE THE SMALL WINS**
Keep an eye out for the little differences you see in yourself and your spouse. Stop and celebrate them in a fun way that's meaningful for you. You could treat yourself to a piece of chocolate or brag them up on social #MenWomenandMoney.

☐ **SCHEDULE A LOOK-BACK ON YOUR CALENDAR**
Mark off 20 minutes in your calendar in the coming week to review your notes, Personal Action Plan, or listen to the audio from the session.

☐ **BUILD YOUR OWN**
You know yourself better than anyone. Write down a specific way you'll overcome the obstacle written in your Personal Action Plan.

SPREAD THE WORD

Did someone you know pop into mind that might really benefit from knowing what you just learned? We're on a mission to help couples do money better together so feel free to **send them a photo of the "Video Rewind" page**.

NOTES

_____

_____

_____

_____

_____

_____

_____

_____

_____

_____

_____

_____

_____

EXTENDED EXPERIENCE

SESSION TWO

WHAT ARE THEY THINKING?

A CASE STUDY

Lexi and Max have been married for 15 years and have a 10-year-old daughter and a 12-year-old son. They have been very intentional about setting financial goals and living within their means. When Max began his career as a realtor, he had to work many long hours and most weekends. Knowing that was what he needed to do to build his business, Lexi was more than willing to be an "almost single parent" to her children when they were younger.

Max has now built a significant client and referral base, and he continues to work late most evenings and many weekends.

Lexi and Max recently moved into their dream house. They enjoy a nice vacation each summer, and have been talking about buying a rental property at a lake to have as a weekend getaway.

Their son is now playing travel baseball and their daughter recently joined a competitive gymnastics team. The family is also involved in their local church. The weekend-intensive schedule has become a source of conflict for Lexi and Max.

This weekend, their daughter has a major gymnastics meet on Saturday morning, and their son's baseball championship tournament is Saturday afternoon and possibly Sunday if his team wins. Max just received a call from a relocation client who will be in town this weekend to shop for a new house. The client is the vice president of a large corporation and it is rumored that the company will be expanding and moving many more of its employees to the area.

Max has agreed to show homes to the client. Lexi is . . . well, let's just say that Lexi is not happy.

Start by putting yourself in the other person's shoes. Answer the questions below, in order. Allow your partner to share their ideas without chiming in. You'll have a chance to talk it through together shortly.

HIS If you were Lexi, what would you have been assuming and thinking during the early years when Max was working nights and weekends away?

HERS If you were Max, what would you have been assuming and thinking during the early years about your growing family, and the lifestyle your wife and kids are beginning to enjoy?

HIS If you were Lexi, what would you have been assuming and thinking as the years went by and Max showed no sign of changing his work schedule? What would you be thinking about the home and the vacations? What would you be thinking about your sense of connectedness?

HERS If you were Max, what would you have been assuming and thinking as the years went by and the lifestyle improved even more? What would you be thinking about the home and the vacations? Your sense of connectedness?

HIS Finally, if you were Lexi, what would you be thinking and feeling in the situation above, and about the choice Max made to show the client the homes?

HERS If you were Max, what would you be thinking and feeling in the situation above, about the client coming in and missing the kids' activities?

Now, return to your own shoes, and share with each other what you would have been thinking in the above scenario, and how you might apply what you've learned.

HERS What would you have been thinking and feeling in the above scenario, from the early years on? What would you be thinking about this weekend? Your home? Vacations? Max's schedule? Your sense of family and connectedness?

HIS What would you have been thinking and feeling in the above scenario, from the early years on? What would you be thinking about this weekend? Your home? Vacations? Your schedule? Your sense of family and connectedness?

HIS Have you had to make a similar decision to Max? If so, did you consider it to be a sacrifice at the time, or just something you had to do? How did you feel about it later?

HERS How might Lexi's current lack of support be affecting Max?

HIS **HERS** When faced with a similar decision (work or family time) in the future, how will you choose? As you talk it through as a couple, what will you consider before making the choice? What changes might each of you want to make going forward?

NOTES

_____

_____

_____

_____

_____

_____

_____

_____

_____

_____

_____

_____

_____

_____

GOING DEEPER

ADDITIONAL DISCUSSION QUESTIONS

If this topic of security is an area of interest or challenge for you, consider continuing your discussion time. Read through the questions and each pick at least one that you would love your partner to answer or discuss.

HERS Have you experienced times when your husband worked especially long hours and/or missed some family time because of his job? What were your assumptions about how he felt not being there? How did his absence affect your feeling of connection?

HIS If you have ever missed family time in that way, was it an easy choice or one you made with regret? If your wife responded differently than you had hoped at the time, what assumptions did you have about her reaction?

HIS Describe how you handle the responsibility of providing for your family. Do you feel pressured or burdened? How might your wife help you feel less pressured?

HERS Do you have spending or saving habits that might threaten your man's sense of security? Understanding that his need to provide for your family is tied to his sense of security, discuss with him how you could increase his feelings of security.

HIS Do you often choose your work and your drive for security over your family? Has there been a cost to this pursuit of financial security? Understanding her need to feel that she is your priority and that you value time with her, how could you increase your wife's feelings of security? Discuss strategies you could implement to make time together a priority.

NOTES

I waited patiently for the Lord; he turned to me and heard my cry. He lifted me out of the slimy pit, out of the mud and mire; he set my feet on a rock and gave me a firm place to stand. He put a new song in my mouth, a hymn of praise to our God. Many will see and fear the Lord and put their trust in him.

PSALM 40:1-3

FAITH FOCUS

BIBLE STUDY

Read the Scripture, and consider the following questions.

1. What does this Scripture tell you about God? List the attributes of God that this passage implies.

2. Think about some moments when you were most troubled by a sense of insecurity, especially about the dynamics we discussed this session (money, providing, time, emotional closeness). In those situations, did you look to anything other than the Lord to get back a sense of security (for example, your job, your bank account, your spouse, your looks, your friends)?

3. What are some challenges that occur when you seek security in those things?

4. What could you have done instead?

5. Look at your list in #1. What does it imply about God's ability to handle those things that make us anxious?

Pause and ask God to grow your faith in him and give you eyes to see the security that comes only from walking closely to him.

NOTES

_____

_____

_____

_____

_____

_____

_____

_____

_____

_____

_____

_____

_____

MAKING MONEY DECISIONS

MEN AND WOMEN PROCESS DECISIONS DIFFERENTLY

SESSION THREE

Since the last session, what have you noticed as you followed up on your Personal Action Plan? What challenged you? In what ways were you successful?

If you are willing, share you observations with your partner or group.

IN THIS SESSION

When it's time to make an important decision, what do you do? Do you get quiet or go someplace to think, where you can consider all of the possibilities—and the consequences? Or is your first instinct to talk about it?

In this session, Jeff and Shaunti will share how research shows men and women process decisions in different ways and on different timelines. You may assume your partner is thinking the same way you do. But that might not be true.

START THE VIDEO FOR THIS LESSON, THEN TAKE NOTES ABOUT WHAT YOU LEARN.
Learn how to access the videos on page 9.

NOT TRUE FOR YOU?

As you will learn, research suggests these patterns are common to most men and women. But there are always exceptions. If your dynamics are different, simply adapt the examples and questions as needed to discuss how these truths apply to you.

**HER BRAIN WIRING
MEANS SHE BEST PROCESSES
THOUGHTS AND FEELINGS
BY TALKING ABOUT THEM.**

— *FOR MEN ONLY*

MEN WHO GO UNDERGROUND

Men who need to think things through before talking them through (especially in a conflict)

Men who don't need to think things through before talking

Adapted from the National Survey of Men: How Men Think 2 for *For Women Only*. Survey data as of January 15, 2005

NOTES ABOUT YOU

_____

_____

_____

_____

_____

_____

_____

_____

YOUR CHECK-IN

TAKE ONE MINUTE TO
REFLECT ON WHAT
YOU JUST LEARNED.

HIS On a scale of 1-10, how true (or not true) is this for you? Do you process things internally? Share an example of how you process things. Try to think of one that is money-related if you can.

HERS Focus and listen as he shares.

WOMEN WHO PROCESS OUT LOUD

When dealing with an emotional situation that requires processing . . .

95%

Women who want to talk it through and value their husband's or partner's input as well as the emotional support they get from being listened to

5%

Women who no longer need to talk it through once their husband or partner suggests a solution

National Survey of Women for *For Men Only.* Survey data as of June 9, 2005

NOTES ABOUT HER

_____

_____

_____

_____

_____

_____

_____

_____

HER CHECK-IN

TAKE ONE MINUTE TO REFLECT ON WHAT YOU JUST LEARNED.

HERS On a scale of 1-10, how true (or not true) is this for you? Do you think things through by talking them through? Share an example of how you process things. Try to think of one that is money-related if you can.

HIS Focus and listen as she shares.

WHAT I CAN DO

WHAT I CAN DO TO SUPPORT MY SPOUSE:

_____

_____

_____

_____

_____

**WHAT I COULD ASK MY PARTNER TO DO THAT
WOULD REALLY HELP ME A LOT:**

_____

_____

_____

_____

_____

MAKING MONEY DECISIONS

VIDEO CONTENT REWIND

In this session, we learned that men and women process thoughts and decisions differently—and money is one of the key areas in which misunderstandings tend to trip us up.

Men are more likely to need time to think through and process their decisions internally, over the course of minutes, hours or even days, depending on the decision. The wiring of the male brain makes it more difficult for men to think things through while talking about them. In fact, the more emotional or important to his wife the decision (like money ones!), the more urgency he may feel to pull away and process it well. The challenge: She may see his withdrawal as uncaring. He is also more likely to verbalize a decision before his wife even knows he's been thinking about it, potentially catching her off guard.

Most women, when faced with a decision or concern, need to think out loud and talk things through. When she hears her husband say his decision out loud, she thinks that he is beginning the conversation, and she begins her verbal processing. As a part of this tendency toward talking things through and her desire for connection, she starts asking questions and making comments for and against the decision. To him, it may seem as if she's challenging his decision.

Thankfully, once we understand each other's processing styles, we can communicate well on any money-related decision, opportunity, or concern that comes up—and grow closer as a result.

BRIGHTPEAK.COM/MENWOMENANDMONEY

DISCUSSION QUESTIONS

These questions are designed to allow you to have a private conversation with your partner, and to gain further insights into how you both think and can apply what you've learned from the chapter. If you are doing this with a group, adapt the questions and exercises as needed. (If a group discussion doesn't lead to you and/or your partner fully understanding what each of you thinks, be sure to continue the conversation later, on your own.)

1. Summarize what you heard from your spouse or significant other during the check-in moments of this video and then communicate it back to him or her. Ask, "Do I have that right?" And give them a chance to elaborate or clarify.

2. Share what you wrote in the "What I could ask my partner to do that would really help me" section.

3. Can you think of a money-related interaction with your partner that illustrates how you process things? Talk about what you were each feeling during that interaction.

4. Knowing what you do now, if you had the opportunity for a do-over on a recent money-related clash, what would you each do differently? How might that have helped avoid the clash?

5. Sometimes couples need to find a tension breaker—a way to signal that emotions are escalating and you need to reset. For example, he might quote a favorite silly song, or she might use the sign language symbol for, "I love you." Together, choose a fun way that you can signal to each other when a discussion is heading for trouble and you need a little pause. (And decide how long the pause will be.)

NOTES

MY PERSONAL ACTION PLAN

Question	Example	Your Response
What do I already do well in this area?	I make sure to give decisions plenty of thoughtful consideration— especially when I know they're important to my wife.	
What do I most need to work on?	I could do a better job bringing her into my process and letting her know that I really am thinking about it.	
What is one short-term action step I can take to get there? Note: This should be something measurable: "Try harder" is not specific!	The next time I'm making a decision that's important to both of us, I'll let her know when I need time to think, and then make time to share together out loud as well.	

PICK ONE WAY TO STAY ON TRACK

brightpeak's behavioral scientists have identified some effective ways for making healthy habits stick.

Pick ONE to do right now. Put an X in the box when you're done.

☐ **GIVE YOURSELF A "TRIGGER"**
Set your phone to ping you at critical times over the next week to remember your Personal Action Plan. This could be before you get home to get you in the right head space, or at the end of the day to reflect on how things went.

☐ **LINE UP SOME SOCIAL SUPPORT**
Take a photo of your Personal Action Plan, text it to a friend and ask them to check-in with you to see how it's going.

☐ **CELEBRATE THE SMALL WINS**
Keep an eye out for the little differences you see in yourself and your spouse. Stop and celebrate them in a fun way that's meaningful for you. You could treat yourself to a piece of chocolate or brag them up on social #MenWomenandMoney.

☐ **SCHEDULE A LOOK-BACK ON YOUR CALENDAR**
Mark off 20 minutes in your calendar in the coming week to review your notes, Personal Action Plan, or listen to the audio from the session.

☐ **BUILD YOUR OWN**
You know yourself better than anyone. Write down a specific way you'll overcome the obstacle written in your Personal Action Plan.

SPREAD THE WORD

Did someone you know pop into mind that might really benefit from knowing what you just learned? We're on a mission to help couples do money better together so feel free to **send them a photo of the "Video Rewind" page**.

NOTES

EXTENDED EXPERIENCE

SESSION THREE

WHAT ARE THEY THINKING?

A CASE STUDY

Kim and Joe have been married for three years and are still paying off heaps of student loans. Kim's car keeps breaking down. In the past six months, Kim and Joe have spent over $1,200 on car repairs. Kim drives 20 miles round trip every day for her job. Meanwhile, Joe travels a lot for his job in a company-provided car. They agree that they need to replace Kim's current car.

Kim would love to buy a new car. Joe's best friend has a well-maintained car for sale. Joe's friend is willing to make a deal and to also finance it. The payment would be $200 a month, no bank needed. Joe comes home and giddily announces that he has found a car and is planning to buy it from his friend this weekend. Joe begins to tell Kim about the car.

Kim begins to ask questions: Has it ever been wrecked? (Yes, but only a minor fender-bender.) How many miles are on it? (95,000.) What kind of gas mileage does it get? (Somewhere around 20-25 mpg highway.) Does it have a USB outlet? (Not sure.) How is it rated for repairs and safety? (Joe's friend says it is well rated.) What color is it? (Blue.) Is it a two-door or four-door? After all, they had been talking about starting a family in the near future. (It's a two-door with a hatch.)

Respond to your respective questions in turn, keeping in mind what you know about processing. Listen carefully to each other's responses to learn more about how your mate thinks.

HERS Put yourself in Joe's shoes. What was he most likely thinking when he decided to buy the car from his friend? What was he expecting from Kim when he told her?

HIS Put yourself in Kim's shoes. Would she have likely been thinking about the car on that long drive to work? (About safety? About the type of car they needed for their future family plans?) What would she have been thinking when Joe came home and shared his plan?

HERS Now step back into a woman's shoes. If you were Kim, what would you have been thinking in this situation? Do you think that Joe's intentions were to help Kim by fixing her broken car problem, or to just take the easy way out by buying a friend's car?

HIS Now step back into a man's shoes. If you were Joe, what would you have been thinking when you decided to buy the car from your friend? Do you think that Joe was being considerate of Kim's needs?

HERS From your perspective, were Kim's questions reasonable to ask Joe? Why or why not? Explain to your partner how you think Kim might have been feeling.

HIS   As Kim began to ask questions, did you think that she was challenging Joe's decision or simply seeking more information? What would it have felt like to be in Joe's shoes when those questions were being raised? Explain how you think Joe might have been feeling.

HIS   **HERS**   What informational blind spots might Kim and Joe have that might have made the conflict worse? Have you ever had a money-related decision where you had a similar breakdown in communication because of similar blind spots? How can you ensure that you communicate well in that type of situation next time it happens?

NOTES

_____

_____

_____

_____

_____

_____

_____

_____

_____

_____

_____

_____

_____

_____

_____

GOING DEEPER

ADDITIONAL DISCUSSION QUESTIONS

In this week's additional discussion questions, we're going to mix it up a little and take turns talking through some questions. She'll go first, and then it will be his turn. As your partner is talking, do your best to stay open and curious. (Remember, you're data gathering.)

HERS Can you think of a recent money-related interaction when you felt your husband suddenly announced a decision that affected you before discussing it with you?

HERS What were some assumptions that you made about your husband and his decision at the time? How did your response reflect those assumptions?

HERS Knowing what you know now, what are some possible factors in his decision-making that he may have handled underground before he filled you in on his decision? Does that change your initial assumptions?

HIS Think back about a situation when your wife did not respond to a money-related decision as you would have wished. Had you previously shared any of your thinking before announcing your decision out loud? Could your process have had something to do with her response?

HIS What underlying assumptions did you have about why she responded in the way that she did (questions, verbalizing her thoughts for and/or against your decision, etc.)? How did those assumptions influence your response?

HIS When a conflict escalates, do you need to pull away farther to think things through? If so, ask her now how you can do so in a way that won't be frustrating for her.

HIS Now that you know about her need to process out loud, how does that help you reframe her responses and better understand her feelings toward you?

NOTES

_____

_____

_____

_____

_____

_____

_____

_____

_____

_____

_____

_____

Therefore, as God's chosen people, holy and dearly loved, clothe yourselves with compassion, kindness, humility, gentleness and patience. Bear with each other and forgive one another if any of you has a grievance against someone. Forgive as the Lord forgave you. And over all these virtues put on love, which binds them all together in perfect unity. Let the peace of Christ rule in your hearts, since as members of one body you were called to peace. And be thankful. Let the message of Christ dwell among you richly as you teach and admonish one another with all wisdom through psalms, hymns, and songs from the Spirit, singing to God with gratitude in your hearts.

COLOSSIANS 3:12-16

FAITH FOCUS

BIBLE STUDY

First, think about a recent money-related disagreement or conflict. Then reread the verse and underline the eight command statements. (Each one starts with an action word. For example, the first is "clothe yourselves with compassion, kindness" and so on.)

Next, spend a few minutes on your own, answering these questions:

1. As you think about how you handle the way your spouse processes things, which of these eight action statements is most true of you—and which do you most need to work on? (For example, perhaps you "bear with" your spouse's processing pattern well, but still need to work on that "being thankful" thing!)

2. Is there anything that you need to apologize for and ask for forgiveness from your spouse?

3. Do you need to show grace and forgiveness to your spouse for anything (even if she does not ask for it)?

NOTES

WINDOWS OF WORRY

MEN AND WOMEN
WORRY DIFFERENTLY

SESSION FOUR

Since the last session, what have you noticed as you followed up on your Personal Action Plan? What challenged you? In what ways were you successful?

If you are willing, share you observations with your partner or group.

IN THIS SESSION

Jeff and Shaunti explain how men and women manage their worries and concerns differently. Since our worries often involve money in some way, understanding each other in this area is crucial for building a great relationship.

START THE VIDEO FOR THIS LESSON, THEN TAKE NOTES ABOUT WHAT YOU LEARN.

Learn how to access the videos on page 9.

NOT TRUE FOR YOU?

As you will learn, research suggests these patterns are common to most men and women. But there are always exceptions. If your dynamics are different, simply adapt the examples and questions as needed to discuss how these truths apply to you.

WOMEN DEAL WITH MULTIPLE THOUGHTS AND EMOTIONS FROM THEIR PAST AND PRESENT ALL THE TIME, AT THE SAME TIME—AND THESE CAN'T BE EASILY DISMISSED.

— FOR MEN ONLY

MEN WHO FEEL LIKE THE WORLD MIGHT STOP SPINNING

"If everyone doesn't pull together and keep things moving forward every single day, things will break down."

80%

20%

I feel like this regularly/ feel like this sometimes.

I rarely or never feel like this.

From the National Survey of How Men Think in the Workplace for *The Male Factor.* Survey data as of September 9, 2008.

NOTES ABOUT YOU

_____

_____

_____

_____

_____

_____

_____

_____

YOUR CHECK-IN

TAKE ONE MINUTE TO REFLECT ON WHAT YOU JUST LEARNED.

HIS On a scale from 1-10 How true (or not true) is this of you? Has there been anything that has made you feel that momentary "are we going to be okay financially?" feeling in the last week? What did you do with that thought?

HERS Focus and listen as he shares.

WOMEN'S OPEN WINDOWS

79%

I deal with many thoughts and emotions at once—it's like having multiple windows open on the computer desktop of my mind.

21%

I mostly think about/ have one window open at a time

National Survey of Women for *For Men Only*. Survey data as of June 9, 2005

NOTES ABOUT HER

_____

_____

_____

_____

_____

_____

_____

HER CHECK-IN

TAKE ONE MINUTE TO REFLECT ON WHAT YOU JUST LEARNED.

HERS On a scale of 1-10 how true (or not true) is this of you? What does it look like for you to use money (spending it or saving it) to close an open window? Example?

HIS Focus and listen as she shares.

WHAT I CAN DO

WHAT I CAN DO TO SUPPORT MY SPOUSE:

_____

_____

_____

_____

_____

**WHAT I COULD ASK MY PARTNER TO DO THAT
WOULD REALLY HELP ME A LOT:**

_____

_____

_____

_____

_____

WINDOWS OF WORRY

VIDEO CONTENT REWIND

In this session, we learned that not only do men and women worry about different things, but how they worry can also be very different. As a result, **both men and women worry about and use money differently.**

A man's brain is a bit like a computer with one window (one thought, one worry), open at a time. As long as the worry is fairly minor, he can compartmentalize and click off thoughts that bother him. That said, one thought that he often feels—even during good financial times—is that he might be just a few steps away from everything falling apart financially. Often looming in the back of his mind is the question, **"Are we going to be okay financially as a family?"** And his insecurities about that can affect other areas of his life. For men, the impact of these financial worries often shows up in a running mental tally of small expenses, withdrawal and frustration.

In contrast, a woman's brain is like a computer with many windows open at once—and she is not able to easily close down a negative thought window that is bothering her. Instead, she usually has to address and resolve the issue in order to close the open window. Because **having an open window is frustrating or even painful,** a woman is usually more willing to spend money to close that window (even if she is more of a saver than a spender).

$\downarrow$

BRIGHTPEAK.COM/MENWOMENANDMONEY

DISCUSSION QUESTIONS

These questions are designed to allow you to have a private conversation with your partner, and to gain further insights into how you both think and can apply what you've learned from the chapter. If you are doing this with a group, adapt the questions and exercises as needed. (If a group discussion doesn't lead to you and/or your partner fully understanding what each of you thinks, be sure to continue the conversation later, on your own.)

1. Summarize what you heard from your spouse or significant other during the check-in moments of this video, and then communicate it back to him or her. Ask, "Do I have that right?" And give them a chance to elaborate or clarify.

2. Share what you wrote in the "What I could ask my partner to do that would really help me" section.

3. In this session, Jeff and Shaunti shared an example of a common money-related disagreement for them: whether to take a child to the doctor. Jeff wanted to wait since the doctor would probably just tell them to "take some Tylenol and call me in the morning." Shaunti wanted to pay to go to the doctor now as a way to close that worry window. How would you have felt in that situation or one like it?

4. Can you think of a money-related interaction that demonstrates how you approach your worries and concerns differently from your spouse?

5. What were you feeling in that interaction? If you had a do-over, how might you handle it differently today?

NOTES

MY PERSONAL ACTION PLAN

Question	Example	Your Response
What do I already do well in this area?	I have noticed that my wife's ability to keep track of many, many things at once far exceeds my ability, and I compliment her on it often.	
What do I most need to work on?	To be more understanding and supportive when she struggles to just let go of a worry.	
What is one short-term action step I can take to get there? Note: This should be something measurable: "Try harder" is not specific!	This week, I will apologize to my wife for not taking her "open windows" seriously enough, and brainstorm ways we can build extra cushion into our budget to accommodate her need to spend money to resolve those windows.	

PICK ONE WAY TO STAY ON TRACK

brightpeak's behavioral scientists have identified some effective ways for making healthy habits stick.

Pick ONE to do right now. Put an X in the box when you're done.

☐ **GIVE YOURSELF A "TRIGGER"**
Set your phone to ping you at critical times over the next week to remember your Personal Action Plan. This could be before you get home to get you in the right head space, or at the end of the day to reflect on how things went.

☐ **LINE UP SOME SOCIAL SUPPORT**
Take a photo of your Personal Action Plan, text it to a friend and ask them to check-in with you to see how it's going.

☐ **CELEBRATE THE SMALL WINS**
Keep an eye out for the little differences you see in yourself and your spouse. Stop and celebrate them in a fun way that's meaningful for you. You could treat yourself to a piece of chocolate or brag them up on social #MenWomenandMoney.

☐ **SCHEDULE A LOOK-BACK ON YOUR CALENDAR**
Mark off 20 minutes in your calendar in the coming week to review your notes, Personal Action Plan, or listen to the audio from the session.

☐ **BUILD YOUR OWN**
You know yourself better than anyone. Write down a specific way you'll overcome the obstacle written in your Personal Action Plan.

SPREAD THE WORD

Did someone you know pop into mind that might really benefit from knowing what you just learned? We're on a mission to help couples do money better together so feel free to **send them a photo of the "Video Rewind" page**

NOTES

EXTENDED
EXPERIENCE

SESSION FOUR

WHAT ARE THEY THINKING?

A CASE STUDY

Abby and Sam have been married for six years, and are hoping to have kids soon. Sam is a restaurant manager, and Abby is a retail store manager. They have some credit card debt and are still paying off a hospital bill from last year when Sam had appendicitis.

Sam's job requires long hours because he is the junior manager. He usually closes the restaurant, working until 1:00 or 2:00 a.m. After having three consecutive years of growth, two new competitors opened and his restaurant's sales have declined this year. Abby is the main manager of her store and can choose the hours she works. She usually opens the store and is done each day by 4:00 p.m.

Abby loves the stability of their jobs and is eager to put down roots. Growing up with a dad in the army, Abby's family moved every two or three years, so it was difficult for Abby to make new friends, and she often would not see her dad for months during deployments. Their apartment lease is set to expire in less than two months and the landlord needs to know whether they are going to renew it. Abby strongly thinks it is time to buy a house.

Abby has been looking online at houses for several months, and recently found an unusually great deal: a wonderful fixer-upper with great potential, in a great school district. She went to see it the same afternoon and asked Sam to look at it with her the next day. She is worried that if they don't move fast, someone else is going to buy it and they will miss the opportunity. Sam is less sure that they should purchase a house right now. He says he doesn't know how much longer he will have a job.

Respond to your respective questions in turn, keeping in mind what you know about processing. Listen carefully to each other's responses to learn more about how your mate thinks.

HERS Put yourself in Sam's shoes. How might he have been feeling in this situation? What was likely on his mind when Abby brought up the fixer-upper idea, knowing that there was a deadline ahead?

HIS Put yourself in Abby's shoes. How might she have been feeling in this situation? How often was she likely thinking about the lease expiring and the possible fixer-upper purchase? Is Abby's desire for the house purely financial? What "windows" might she be trying to close with the purchase? What might she be feeling about Sam's concerns?

HERS If you were Abby, what would be going through your mind in this situation?

HIS If you were Sam, imagine how you would be thinking and feeling in this situation. How might you respond?

HIS HERS What can Sam and Abby do to resolve their conflicting needs in this time-sensitive situation? What can Sam do to help Abby close her open windows regarding their home? What can Abby do to better support Sam's insecurities? How can they unite together to bring closure to their concerns?

HIS HERS Have you ever been in a money-related situation with big worries that were exacerbated by a deadline or time urgency? What were you each feeling in that situation? Knowing what you know now, how might you handle it differently in the future?

GOING DEEPER

ADDITIONAL DISCUSSION QUESTIONS

If this topic of windows and worries is an area of interest or challenge for you, consider continuing your discussion time with these additional questions.

HERS Can you think of a money-related thought that you had difficulty releasing or closing down until it was resolved? What made it more difficult to close than other worries?

HERS In that situation (or others like it), what could your spouse have said or done that would have helped you (or did help you) move past the worry?

HIS Can you recall a seemingly minor situation that triggered a financial doom and gloom response from you? (Hearing about your colleague's recent promotion, seeing your wife's shopping bags, hearing that your company's sales numbers have dropped?) What were you feeling at the time? How did your partner respond, and how do you wish she would respond to similar situations in the future?

HERS In the situation he recalls (or a similar one), did you feel at the time that his response seemed unwarranted, overblown or confusing? Describe what you were assuming at the time. Discuss how the two of you can address such situations in the future so that both your needs and concerns are honored.

NOTES

Therefore, I tell you, do not worry about your life, what you will eat or drink; or about your body, what you will wear. Is not life more than food, and the body more than clothes? Look at the birds of the air; they do not sow or reap or store away in barns, and yet your heavenly Father feeds them. Are you not much more valuable than they? Can any one of you by worrying add a single hour to your life?

MATTHEW 6:25-27

FAITH FOCUS

BIBLE STUDY

1. The first sentence in the Scripture above is a command: "Do not worry" about how you will make ends meet. We think of worries as insidious thoughts that are essentially outside of our control. What does Jesus' command imply?

2. In matters of provision, our human nature tends to want to control. We want security. We want to know we have enough money in the bank and food on the table. And yet looking at the last sentence in the Scripture above, what does it say about whether our worries themselves accomplish anything?

Do Jesus' words instruct us to do nothing "practical?" Or is the instruction more about the position of our hearts?

3. Look at the second half of verse 25: "Is not life more than . . . ?" What is life, according to Jesus, if it is "more than" seeking after provision? How might seeking provision prevent finding the "more than?"

4. In what ways do Jesus' words comfort you in your worries?

5. As a couple, how can you pray for each other and support each other through your times of worry? Spend a few minutes and write a prayer that you can both pray to comfort and remind you that God is for you and that he will provide. Pray for help in growing your trust and faith that he will answer your prayer, even when it does not seem possible. Pray for peace and comfort and the ability to rest in that knowledge. And most importantly, thank him for all that he has given to you.

Finally, say this prayer together. Make a copy of it and keep it with you so that you can repeat it whenever needed.

NOTES

KNOWING WHEN TO JUST LISTEN

MEN AND WOMEN NEED TO BE SUPPORTED DIFFERENTLY

SESSION FIVE

Since the last session, what have you noticed as you followed up on your Personal Action Plan? What challenged you? In what ways were you successful?

If you are willing, share you observations with your partner or group.

IN THIS SESSION

In this session, we'll learn what listening means to our spouse—because it is often quite different than we might think. Learning to listen is crucial when our partner is sharing dreams or concerns, especially since those dreams or concerns are often money-related! So watch the video now—and listen up!

START THE VIDEO FOR THIS LESSON, THEN TAKE NOTES ABOUT WHAT YOU LEARN.

Learn how to access the videos on page 9.

NOT TRUE FOR YOU?

As you will learn, research suggests these patterns are common to most men and women. But there are always exceptions. If your dynamics are different, simply adapt the examples and questions as needed to discuss how these truths apply to you.

WHEN SHE IS SHARING AN EMOTIONAL PROBLEM, HER FEELINGS AND HER DESIRE TO BE HEARD ARE MUCH MORE IMPORTANT THAN THE [ACTUAL] PROBLEM ITSELF.

— *FOR MEN ONLY*

HE LIKES TO DREAM

79%

of men said they
enjoyed emotionally
investing in a dream
or passion outside the
boundaries of work and
everyday life.

63%

of men said they
enjoyed it because it
offered an alternate
reality—an escape
from everyday
responsibilities.

National Survey of Men: How Men Think 2 for *For Women Only*. Survey data as of January 15, 2005 Paraphrased; Unpublished data

NOTES ABOUT YOU

_____

_____

_____

_____

_____

_____

_____

_____

YOUR CHECK-IN

TAKE ONE MINUTE TO
REFLECT ON WHAT
YOU JUST LEARNED.

HIS On a scale from 1-10, how true (or not true) is this of you? Share an example of how you dream out loud or think, "Wouldn't it be great if we _____" thoughts.

HERS Focus and listen as he shares.

SHE DOESN'T NEED A FIXER—SHE NEEDS A LISTENER

95% of women said that when their partner listens briefly and then offers a reasonable solution to their emotional issue (like a conflict with a close friend) it doesn't solve the real problem.

60% said they just want you to listen to how they are feeling.

From the National Survey of Women for *For Men Only*. Survey data as of June 9, 2005

NOTES ABOUT HER

_____

_____

_____

_____

_____

_____

_____

_____

HER CHECK-IN

TAKE ONE MINUTE TO REFLECT ON WHAT YOU JUST LEARNED.

▬▬▬▬▬▬▬

HERS On a scale of 1-10 how true (or not true) is this of you? Are there times when you share a problem and just want him to listen to your feelings?

HIS Focus and listen as she shares.

WHAT I CAN DO

WHAT I CAN DO TO SUPPORT MY SPOUSE:

_____

_____

_____

_____

_____

**WHAT I COULD ASK MY PARTNER TO DO THAT
WOULD REALLY HELP ME A LOT:**

_____

_____

_____

_____

KNOWING WHEN TO JUST LISTEN

VIDEO CONTENT REWIND

The teaching this week focused on just how different our listening needs are as men and women. **There are times that both of us want the other to just listen.** In other words, we want our spouse or significant other to enter into what we're thinking or feeling without analysis or solutions. But the situations that trigger that desire tend to be polar opposites. And since they often involve money matters in some way, listening becomes crucial. Otherwise, we can cause hurt that neither of us intended.

Men need the freedom to dream even crazy dreams out loud, while knowing that they may not be about to pick up and act on those dreams. And nearly all such dreams have a money implication. A man knows the drawbacks and fallacies, but the dream becomes an escape—and one he wants to share with you. So the next time he suggests taking a year off and operating a charter fishing boat on a Caribbean island, don't panic (or point out that he gets seasick in the bathtub). Just listen. **Dreaming refuels his emotional capacity to face his real-life obstacles and challenges.**

When a woman talks about an emotional problem, she is often processing out loud (remember Session 3?), and the specific things she is processing out loud right now are her feelings about the situation. While men are wired to try to fix it, this is a time to instead focus on understanding her feelings and helping her talk through them. So the next time she is upset that her sister gossiped and told their mother something she said in confidence, stop yourself from suggesting that she call her sister right away. **Just listen to how she's feeling, and ask questions about it.** She will feel validated and loved.

BRIGHTPEAK.COM/MENWOMENANDMONEY

DISCUSSION QUESTIONS

1. Summarize what you heard from your spouse or significant other during the check-in moments of this video, and then communicate it back to him or her. Ask, "Do I have that right?" And give them a chance to elaborate or clarify.

2. Share what you wrote in the "What I could ask my partner to do that would really help me" section.

3. In this session, Jeff and Shaunti shared the example of a man who dreams of restoring a 1965 Mustang, and a woman who might immediately start thinking (or saying), "But what about . . . ?" Try to think of a money-related example where one of you was dreaming out loud and the other started poking holes. In that example, did those, "But what about?" questions need to be raised? If so, how can the dreamer be heard, while the analyst still feels able to raise issues that need to be raised? If not, how could the analyst better let the dreamer dream?

4. As described, women tend to need their feelings to be heard, while men sometimes feel that it's a bit wimpy, or even uncaring to just listen and not help. But ironically, jumping in with a solution can feel uncaring to her. If those dynamics are true in your relationship, talk about a recent example (money-related or not) where this happened. Describe for each other what you felt, were hoping for, and/or were trying to accomplish.

5. In that situation, what could each of you have done differently for a better outcome?

6. Can you think of a money-related interaction with your spouse where they did listen in a way that made you feel heard? If so, share it so they know what would be helpful to replicate.

NOTES

MY PERSONAL ACTION PLAN

Question	Example	Your Response
What do I already do well in this area?	I work hard to listen to her and let her talk before responding.	
What do I most need to work on?	I need to figure out when she just wants to talk and when she really would like help with a solution.	
What is one short-term action step I can take to get there? Note: This should be something measurable: "Try harder" is not specific!	When she begins sharing a problem, I will ask questions to draw out her feelings, and also ask, "Do you want any feedback right now, or do you mostly want a sounding board?"	

PICK ONE WAY TO STAY ON TRACK

brightpeak's behavioral scientists have identified some effective ways for making healthy habits stick.

Pick ONE to do right now. Put an X in the box when you're done.

☐ **GIVE YOURSELF A "TRIGGER"**
Set your phone to ping you at critical times over the next week to remember your Personal Action Plan. This could be before you get home to get you in the right head space, or at the end of the day to reflect on how things went.

☐ **LINE UP SOME SOCIAL SUPPORT**
Take a photo of your Personal Action Plan, text it to a friend and ask them to check-in with you to see how it's going.

☐ **CELEBRATE THE SMALL WINS**
Keep an eye out for the little differences you see in yourself and your spouse. Stop and celebrate them in a fun way that's meaningful for you. You could treat yourself to a piece of chocolate or brag them up on social #MenWomenandMoney.

☐ **SCHEDULE A LOOK-BACK ON YOUR CALENDAR**
Mark off 20 minutes in your calendar in the coming week to review your notes, Personal Action Plan, or listen to the audio from the session.

☐ **BUILD YOUR OWN**
You know yourself better than anyone. Write down a specific way you'll overcome the obstacle written in your Personal Action Plan.

SPREAD THE WORD

Did someone you know pop into mind that might really benefit from knowing what you just learned? We're on a mission to help couples do money better together so feel free to **send them a photo of the "Video Rewind" page**.

NOTES

_____

_____

_____

_____

_____

_____

_____

_____

_____

_____

_____

_____

_____

_____

EXTENDED
EXPERIENCE

WHAT ARE THEY THINKING?

A CASE STUDY

Carolina is at her wit's end. She took this cashier job so that their family could have some extra money to go on a real vacation to the beach. If they save all of her pay for the next few months, they can afford to get a condo on the beach. They haven't had a vacation since their twins were born 5 years ago. But lately, Carolina's boss keeps changing her hours at the last minute, and she has to rush to rearrange childcare to go in early because several co-workers have been sick. Today, she gets home from a particularly hard shift and sees Bart thumbing through a Mediterranean cruise pamphlet and highlighting all of the stops.

Bart looks up from the pamphlet. "Hey, babe! Look what came in the mail. This would be so much fun someday." Carolina glowers. Bart quickly figures out something is wrong and follows up with, "Ummm, is something wrong?" Carolina begins unloading about her boss and the rude customer that she waited on and . . .

Bart interrupts. "Honey, this job is not worth this stress. Why don't you quit and we will figure out some other vacation?"

Carolina shrieks, "Good grief! Just forget I ever said anything." She grabs the dog and his leash and goes for a long walk. Bart looks wistfully at the cruise pamphlet and throws it in the trash. Then he sits down in the chair to try to figure out what just happened and what to do next.

Put yourselves in the other person's shoes as you consider these questions.

`HERS` What was Bart thinking when he brought up the cruise? What was he looking for?

`HIS` What was Carolina probably feeling that day at her difficult job?

`HERS` What was Bart likely thinking as Carolina started unloading about her job?

`HIS` What might she have thought when Bart suggested that she quit?

`HERS` What do you think motivated Bart to suggest that Carolina quit her job? How might that suggestion also impact him?

`HIS` Was there anything that Bart could have done differently to better support his wife?

`HERS` Was there anything Carolina could have done differently?

`HIS` `HERS` Now, switch back to your own shoes. Imagine what you each think you would have been feeling in this situation. Give feedback to your partner on their guesses. How did you do at your own guesses?

`HIS` `HERS` Did you learn anything new about your partner from hearing what they would have been thinking? If so, summarize it here.

`HIS` `HERS` In a few minutes, Carolina will come back in from walking the dog. What could each of them do at this point?

`HIS` `HERS` How can you apply your learning from this session to your own listening and communication with each other in the future?

GOING DEEPER

ADDITIONAL DISCUSSION QUESTIONS

If this topic of listening is an area of interest or challenge for you, continue your discussion time. Pick at least one question that you want your partner to answer.

HERS How does your husband's or boyfriend's listening to your problem without providing a solution help you? In other words: Is "just listening" actually a solution on its own? How so? When he does that, how does that make you feel about him?

HERS When sharing a concern with him, how can you signal whether you want him to simply listen to your feelings or whether you're seeking input from him?

HIS Can you remember a time when you shared a "just dreaming out loud" moment with your wife or girlfriend? In your mind, what was different about these dreams from your more usual discussions of actual future planning? How can your partner tell the difference between a dreaming moment, when you want her to just listen and not analyze, and a concrete future-planning moment, which requires some back-and-forth?

HIS Sometimes, a wife might worry that her act of entering in to a dream with you, just for fun, might encourage you to do something crazy because you think she's in full agreement. If she dreamed with you, would that make you want to suddenly go for it? And if you did, how could she move to analysis mode without stomping on your dream?

HIS **HERS** When your partner dreams with you and offers encouragement (even when you know your dream isn't realistic), how does it make you feel? What if she didn't encourage you? What assumptions would you make if she wasn't encouraging?

HIS **HERS** Going forward, how can what you've learned about listening help you handle your next money decision differently?

NOTES

_____

_____

_____

_____

_____

_____

_____

_____

_____

_____

_____

You must all be quick to listen, slow
to speak, and slow to get angry.

JAMES 1:19 NLT

To answer before listening—that is
folly and shame.

PROVERBS 18:13

Making your ear attentive to
wisdom and inclining your heart to
understanding.

PROVERBS 2:2 ESV

FAITH FOCUS

BIBLE STUDY

1. According to these verses, what are some of the consequences of not listening? What are the consequences of listening? Have you seen the truth of these in action in your life? Share an example.

2. What do you think being quick to listen has to do with being slow to speak or get angry?

3. Look at James 1:19 in context by reading verses 19-27. What does James say will happen if we are quick to listen? For example, look at verse 20: If anger does not produce righteousness, do verses 19-20 together imply that listening will help produce something else? How?

4. Knowing that the Bible is our instruction manual from God, choose one or two of these verses and rewrite them as a personalized instruction to yourself. (For example, "Jeff, you must be quick to listen, slow to speak and slow to become angry.")

5. How does that change the importance of these verses for you? What specifically can you do differently to do what God has asked you to do?

NOTES

FILLING THEIR TANK

MEN AND WOMEN FEEL APPRECIATED DIFFERENTLY

SESSION SIX

Since the last session, what have you noticed as you followed up on your Personal Action Plan? What challenged you? In what ways were you successful?

If you are willing, share you observations with your partner or group.

IN THIS SESSION

We all make mistakes. And we all have little individual quirks that can cause conflict with our spouse or significant other—especially when it comes to money. In this last session of the series, Jeff and Shaunti share what we can do to build goodwill—not just because we care, but also because it will help our partner have grace with our slipups when they occur.

START THE VIDEO FOR THIS LESSON, THEN TAKE NOTES ABOUT WHAT YOU LEARN.

Learn how to access the videos on page 9.

NOT TRUE FOR YOU?

As you will learn, research suggests these patterns are common to most men and women. But there are always exceptions. If your dynamics are different, simply adapt the examples and questions as needed to discuss how these truths apply to you.

REMEMBER: FOR WOMEN,
THERE IS NEVER A MAGIC
MOMENT OF CLOSURE WHEN
THEY FEEL PERMANENTLY,
FULLY, DEEPLY LOVED. THEY
THINK THAT'S WHAT THE REST
OF MARRIED LIFE IS FOR!
— *FOR MEN ONLY*

"THANK YOU" TO A MAN IS LIKE "I LOVE YOU" TO A WOMAN

98% of men say it fills them up emotionally when their wife notices what they do and sincerely thanks them for it—for example, "Thank you for mowing the lawn."

From the National Survey of Men: How Men Think for *For Women Only*. Survey data as of November 17, 2003

NOTES ABOUT YOU

_____

_____

_____

_____

_____

_____

_____

_____

YOUR CHECK-IN

TAKE ONE MINUTE TO REFLECT ON WHAT YOU JUST LEARNED.

HIS Jeff and Shaunti shared research about what daily actions help a man feel appreciated and build up goodwill with him. How true (or not true) is that for you? Is it easier to have grace with your wife when she has been showing you daily that she cares?

HERS Focus and listen as he shares.

"YOU'RE BEAUTIFUL" ARE MAGIC WORDS

Do women have a deep need or desire to know that their significant other finds them beautiful?

77%

23%

"Yes . . . on the inside, I'm still like that little girl who wants to hear that she's beautiful."

"No, I don't have that need."

From the National Survey of Women for *For Men Only*. Survey data as of June 9, 2005 (Women age 45 and younger)

NOTES ABOUT HER

_____

_____

_____

_____

_____

_____

_____

_____

HER CHECK-IN

TAKE ONE MINUTE TO REFLECT ON WHAT YOU JUST LEARNED.

HERS Jeff and Shaunti shared research about what daily actions help a woman feel loved, and build up goodwill with her. How true (or not true) is that for you? Is it easier to overlook your man's financial quirks when he's been making you feel cared for every day?

HIS Focus and listen as she shares.

WHAT I CAN DO

WHAT I CAN DO TO SUPPORT MY SPOUSE:

_____

_____

_____

_____

_____

**WHAT I COULD ASK MY PARTNER TO DO THAT
WOULD REALLY HELP ME A LOT:**

_____

_____

_____

_____

_____

FILLING THEIR TANK

VIDEO CONTENT REWIND

Each of us has some very individual money quirks—ways we handle money that could otherwise drive our spouse a bit crazy. **But when we focus on doing the little daily things that make our partners feel constantly loved and appreciated, it builds up a reservoir of goodwill.** They are more likely to have grace with us. And we create the type of relationship in which it is easier to have grace with them.

The key to making a man feel cared for starts with recognizing the hidden insecurity inside—showing that you appreciate him and that he makes you happy. "Thank you" is powerful.

The key to making a woman feel deeply cared for starts with recognizing her subconscious doubts about whether she is enough to hold you—showing her that you love being married to her. Small physical gestures of affection, or sending her a sweet text during the day, are therefore not small at all—they are quite meaningful.

Over time, these simple gestures create for our loved one a foundation of knowing that we care when our inevitable quirks appear or we slip up (and we will!); our partner is better able to handle it in a healthy manner without triggering resentment or insecurity.

The word *appreciate* means, "to recognize the full worth of." As we go forward in our love and money relationship, remember that **our partners need to feel appreciated by us every single day.** Our spouse is our most priceless gift: one that can never be replaced by money. If we appreciate our mate daily and build up our relational bank account, we will see our marriage—and how we handle money together—flourish.

BRIGHTPEAK.COM/MENWOMENANDMONEY

DISCUSSION QUESTIONS

1. Summarize what you heard from your partner during the check-in moments of this video, then ask, "Do I have that right?" Give them a chance to elaborate or clarify.

2. Share what you wrote in the "What I could ask my partner to do that would really help me" section.

3. Session 1 covered underlying insecurities, and the related need of men to feel respected and women to feel loved. In the past few weeks, have you seen examples of your partner's insecurity that you had not noticed before? How can this awareness help you be more intentional in building goodwill with them? How can it help you show grace when they need it?

4. In the story about Katie and Sasha's trip, Katie's husband was more understanding than Sasha's—in part because of what each did (or didn't do) to build goodwill. Give examples of daily actions that each woman might have done to create goodwill or damage it.

5. Imagine the Katie and Sasha scenario in reverse: that it was the husbands who encountered an unexpected major expense, and one marriage had a reservoir of goodwill, while the other did not. Give examples of daily actions that each husband has been doing to create or damage goodwill.

6. Imagine that this sort of situation had played out in your relationship. What might the outcome have been? Which couple could you most relate to? If you are not happy with your answer, what can you do differently?

7. What can you do differently to build goodwill? Do you think that will make a difference the next time one of you has a money mistake or is impacted by the other person's money foibles?

NOTES

MY PERSONAL ACTION PLAN

Question	Example	Your Response
What do I already do well in this area?	Whenever she dresses up, I tell her she is beautiful.	
What do I most need to work on?	Making her feel special and not taken for granted every day—not just on special occasions.	
What is one short-term action step I can take to get there? Note: This should be something measurable: "Try harder" is not specific!	For the next month, I will hug her before I leave for work and tell her something like, "I can't wait to see you tonight."	

PICK ONE WAY TO STAY ON TRACK

brightpeak's behavioral scientists have identified some effective ways for making healthy habits stick.

Pick ONE to do right now. Put an X in the box when you're done.

☐ **GIVE YOURSELF A "TRIGGER"**
Set your phone to ping you at critical times over the next week to remember your Personal Action Plan. This could be before you get home to get you in the right head space, or at the end of the day to reflect on how things went.

☐ **LINE UP SOME SOCIAL SUPPORT**
Take a photo of your Personal Action Plan, text it to a friend and ask them to check in with you to see how it's going.

☐ **CELEBRATE THE SMALL WINS**
Keep an eye out for the little differences you see in yourself and your spouse. Stop and celebrate them in a fun way that's meaningful for you. You could treat yourself to a piece of chocolate or brag them up on social #MenWomenandMoney.

☐ **SCHEDULE A LOOK-BACK ON YOUR CALENDAR**
Mark off 20 minutes in your calendar in the coming week to review your notes, Personal Action Plan, or listen to the audio from the session.

☐ **BUILD YOUR OWN**
You know yourself better than anyone. Write down a specific way you'll overcome the obstacle written in your Personal Action Plan.

SPREAD THE WORD

Did someone you know pop into mind that might really benefit from knowing what you just learned? We're on a mission to help couples do money better together so feel free to **send them a photo of the "Video Rewind" page.**

KEEP THE MOMENTUM GOING
MY PERSONAL ACTION PLAN

Question	Example	Your Response
Looking back at everything you've learned from these six sessions, what are the most important changes you have made that you want to be sure to keep going in the months to come?	I have been much better about prioritizing family time, to show my wife that I'm prioritizing her.	
What is the one most important new change you want to pursue in the months to come?	I need to listen to her feelings, especially about money worries, without feeling criticized and shutting down.	

BRIGHTPEAK.COM/MENWOMENANDMONEY

STAYING ON TRACK IN THE MONTHS AHEAD

SET A STANDING TIME TO REVIEW THIS BOOK

You now have your personalized guidebook for doing money as a couple, and it will always be here for you to refer back to when things get hard. Even better than waiting until the stress builds is to set a standing time to review and remember what you've learned, and think through how you can keep applying it as a couple.

KEEP THE MOMENTUM GOING WITH TOGETHER™

brightpeak has created a free online love and money coach designed to support couples in taking sustained action toward improving their relationships and their finances. In Together™ you'll find free assessments, relationship and financial tools, as wells as fun challenges. Jeff and Shaunti have even created a challenge for you to help you keep your momentum going.

brightpeak.com/JeffandShauntiChallenge

UNTIL NEXT TIME

On behalf of Jeff, Shaunti, brightpeak and everyone who poured their hearts into bringing this material to life, thank you.

Thank you for caring enough about your partner and your marriage to challenge yourselves to work together to learn some new tools. Thank you for trusting us and allowing us to speak into your lives.

Our prayer is that this is the beginning of a whole new chapter in your family's story, and we look forward to supporting you along the way.

NOTES

NOTES

_____

_____

_____

_____

_____

_____

_____

_____

_____

_____

_____

_____

_____

_____

_____

EXTENDED
EXPERIENCE

WHAT ARE THEY THINKING?

A CASE STUDY

Stephen and Rebecca married in their early 30's. Before marriage, Rebecca had been carefree with her spending and not worried about paying more than the minimum balance each month. She confessed her financial troubles to Stephen and they worked out a strict plan to pay everything off in three years. She slipped up every now and then, but worked hard to make things right. They paid off all but one credit card and a small student loan, and were anxious to get a credit score high enough to buy a house.

Suddenly, Rebecca's mom got very sick with an illness that required a lot of time from Rebecca. Practically living between her mom's house and the hospital for the month, she completely forgot to pay her credit card bill, car payment and the electric bill. On top of that, she put $150 in new department store charges on the credit card.

When Stephen opened the mail one day and all four bills showed up—with late fees and interest—he was livid. Rebecca had promised that she would no longer use the credit card and would pay her bills on time.

And then he paused. She had been working her full-time job and caring for her mom. Despite all of that, she had somehow managed to always be patient with his long hours at work, and had even thrown him a 35th birthday party. She had proven her commitment to getting out of debt. There must be more to the story.

Stephen texted Rebecca about it, and Rebecca called him back in tears. Not only had she forgotten to pay the regular bills, but she had purchased some clothes for her mom as an early birthday present and had put it on the credit card "just this once" for convenience.

She was upset with herself and expected Stephen to be angry, too. But he responded, "It's okay, babe. You have had a lot on your plate and I know how hard you have been working on this. This was simply a mistake."

**One goal of the case study exercise for the previous
five sessions was learning how the other person thinks
in order to build empathy and understanding. In this
final session, take the next step, as a way of building
goodwill: Take turns responding and listening.**

HERS How do you think Rebecca felt when she realized
her mistake? How do you think she felt when Stephen
showed grace and did not get upset with her? Do you
think this motivated her or demotivated her to continue
to work on paying off the bills—even though they had a
setback on their credit scores?

HIS If you were Stephen, how difficult would it have
been for you to stop yourself from assuming that Rebecca
had lost her focus on paying the bills? Would you have
thought that she'd done it on purpose? What do you think
prompted Stephen to pause and not jump to conclusions?

HIS **HERS** How might Stephen and Rebecca's
relationship change as a result of this interaction? Who do
you think benefited the most?

HIS **HERS** What did Rebecca do that allowed
Stephen to pause when faced with potentially damaging
information? How can you, like Stephen, remember to
pause before jumping to blame your partner, and give
him or her the benefit of the doubt instead?

GOING DEEPER

ADDITIONAL DISCUSSION QUESTIONS

HERS What are two or three little daily actions/words that your husband could use to help you feel more secure in his love?

HIS What are two or three little daily actions/words that help you feel most respected and appreciated by your wife?

HIS **HERS** Can you think of a money-related interaction with your partner when goodwill and grace was needed in your relationship? Were you able to work through it easily? Or was it a challenging interaction? If so, what could you have done differently?

HIS **HERS** Think of a difficulty in your relationship that you have experienced over and over, but that you now better understand through this series. Fill in the following blanks and share it with each other: In the past whenever you [did/did not do] this _____ _____, I interpreted it as you did not [respect/love] me. From these lessons, I have realized that what you were actually doing/saying was _____ _____. Is that correct?

HERS Think back to recent conversations that you have shared with your friends or family members. Have your words or stories demonstrated your respect for your partner? Or have there been instances when you conveyed disrespect without realizing it? Do you think it matters whether you convey disrespect when he's not there to hear it? What are some ways that you can convey respect to him through your conversations with others?

HIS Think back to some interactions you've had with your partner, especially when you disagreed about something. Did your words or actions demonstrate love (even when you might not have been feeling it)? Do you think that you should give unconditional love (even when she is unlovable) just as you crave unconditional respect? What are some ways you can communicate your love to her even when you're feeling angry or frustrated?

NOTES

_____

_____

_____

_____

_____

_____

_____

_____

_____

_____

_____

Bear with each other and forgive one another if any of you has a grievance against someone. Forgive as the Lord forgave you. And over all these virtues put on love, which binds them all together in perfect unity.

COLOSSIANS 3:13–14

Therefore encourage one another and build each other up, just as in fact you are doing.

1 THESSALONIANS 5:11

FAITH FOCUS

BIBLE STUDY

1. Read the verses on the previous page. How do they apply in situations where either you or your spouse has a money-related quirk that frustrates the other, or makes an actual money-related mistake? Are there any conditions to when and how these commands apply?

2. What do you think is the relationship between "bearing with" each other and forgiving each other? Are they the same thing? Or does one choice enable the other?

Indeed, we all make many mistakes. For if we could control our tongues, we would be perfect and could also control ourselves in every other way. We can make a large horse go wherever we want by means of a small bit in its mouth. And a small rudder makes a huge ship turn wherever the pilot chooses to go, even though the winds are strong. In the same way, the tongue is a small thing that makes grand speeches. But a tiny spark can set a great forest on fire. . . . And so blessing and cursing come pouring out of the same mouth. Surely, my brothers and sisters, this is not right!
JAMES 3:2-5; 10 NLT

3. Now carefully read the verses from James. What does this say is the key to controlling ourselves? What does this imply about what we are capable of doing when we are provoked by our spouse's money foibles? What should we do?

4. How do these verses apply to doing the little day-to-day things that will make our spouses feel cared for and build up goodwill? How does this apply to the little things that might make our spouse feel that we do not care for them? According to these verses, then, what is the key to success?

Do not judge others, and you will not be judged. For you will be treated as you treat others. The standard you use in judging is the standard by which you will be judged. . . . If you sinful people know how to give good gifts to your children, how much more will your heavenly Father give good gifts to those who ask him. Do to others whatever you would like them to do to you. This is the essence of all that is taught in the law and the prophets.
MATTHEW 7:1–2; 11–12 NLT

5. Think of a time when you made a mistake related to money, whether your realized it at the time or not. Perhaps you overspent, paid a bill late or purchased something extravagant without consulting your spouse. When you realized your mistake, how did you want your spouse to respond?

Now, think of a time when your spouse made a mistake related to money. How did you respond? How did your response to their mistake compare with the response you wished you'd gotten from them for yours? If you did respond as you would have wanted, what were the key factors that led to that success? If not, what would allow you to have more success next time?

6. In thinking through your responses to the questions above, is there anything for which you need to forgive your spouse? Anything you need to ask for forgiveness about?

NOTES

NOTES

SESSION # 1 - You Hit a Nerve
   "Even women . . . ," *For Men Only*, 24.

SESSION # 2 - Homeland Security
   "Women feel secure . . . ," *For Men Only*, 97.

SESSION # 3 - Making Money Decisions
   "Her brain wiring . . . ," *For Men Only*, 123.

SESSION # 4 - Windows of Worry
   "Women deal with multiple . . . ," *For Men Only*, 41.

SESSION # 5 - Knowing When to Just Listen
   "When she is sharing an emotional problem . . . ," *For Men Only*, 9.

SESSION # 6 - Filling Their Tank
   "Remember: For women . . . ," *For Men Only*, 36.

RESOURCES

Feldhahn, Shaunti and Jeff. *For Men Only: A Straightforward Guide to the Inner Lives of Women, Revised and Updated Edition.* Colorado Springs: Multnomah, 2006, 2013.

Feldhahn, Shaunti. *For Women Only: What You Need to Know About the Inner Lives of Men, Revised and Updated Edition.* Colorado Springs: Multnomah, 2004, 2013.

Feldhahn, Shaunti. *The Male Factor: The Unwritten Rules, Misperceptions, and Secret Beliefs of Men in the Workplace.* New York: Broadway Books, 2009.

Feldhahn, Shaunti, and Robert Lewis. *The Life Ready Woman: Thriving in a Do-It-All World.* Nashville: B & H Publishing Group, 2011, 2017.

Feldhahn, Shaunti. *The Surprising Secrets of Highly Happy Marriages: The Little Things That Make a Big Difference.* Colorado Springs: Multnomah, 2013.

Other Books by
Shaunti Feldhahn and Jeff Feldhahn

For Men Only: A Straightforward Guide
to the Inner Lives of Women

For Young Men Only: A Guy's Guide to the Alien
Gender (coauthored with Eric Rice)

OTHER NONFICTION BOOKS BY SHAUNTI FELDHAHN

Find Rest: A Women's Devotional for Lasting Peace in a Busy Life

For Parents Only

For Women Only in the Workplace

For Women Only: What You Need to Know
About the Inner Lives of Men

For Young Women Only

Made to Crave for Young Women
(coauthored with Lysa TerKeurst)

The Good News about Marriage

The Kindness Challenge

The Life Ready Woman

The Male Factor

The Surprising Secrets of Highly Happy Marriages

Through a Man's Eyes: Helping Women Understand the Visual
Nature of Men
(coauthored with Craig Gross)

FICTION BOOKS BY SHAUNTI FELDHAHN

The Veritas Conflict

The Lights on Tenth Street

Shaunti and Jeff Feldhahn are best-selling authors, popular speakers and nationally renowned social researchers. Fifteen years ago this average couple stumbled over some things they just didn't "get" about each other. They have used their analytical backgrounds ever since to help other semi-confused couples decode each other. Both with graduate degrees from Harvard, Shaunti and Jeff are the authors and coauthors of many groundbreaking books, such as *For Women Only* and *For Men Only*.

As the primary researcher, Shaunti is always in the middle of her next research project, while attorney-entrepreneur Jeff is always in the middle of his next technology company start-up. The Feldhahns have two children and live in Atlanta, Georgia.

brightpeak

WHO WE ARE

brightpeak, a division of Thrivent Financial, is a not-for-profit membership organization that helps Christian couples grow stronger in their relationship with one another by offering products, tools and resources that help them improve the way they co-manage their finances. We are the only organization that offers a holistic approach to helping individuals achieve financial confidence and strength, resulting in changed lives, stronger communities and a better world.

WHO WE'RE FOR

We're for the people who want transparency and honesty in a company. We're for the people who work hard for their paychecks and need their money to go to work for them. We're for the moms and dads who put their families first, and want to balance simplicity with effectiveness in their finances.

www.brightpeak.com